The Australian Aborigines

B. A. L. Cranstone

The Australian Aborigines

Published by the Trustees of the British Museum
London 1973

(*Front cover*)
A man of the cockatoo totem decorated
for a ceremony; Arnhem Land.
From a photograph by Axel Poignant

(*Frontispiece*)
A section of a large group of paintings
in a rock shelter in the Laura District,
inland of Cooktown, northern
Queensland. They include human and
spirit figures, animals, plants, utensils,
and other subjects. These paintings show
many examples of relative dating by
superimposition. The large white ibis
and the human figure with raised arms
are superimposed on the snake and are
therefore more recent. The snake in turn
covers part of the head of the human
figure next to the ibis, the right arm of
which is covered by the ibis. The
boomerang (*top*) is more recent than
the fish (in 'X-ray' style) beneath it.

SBN 7141 1535 5

©The Trustees of the British Museum
Printed in Great Britain
by Lund Humphries

Prepared by
the Ethnography Department
at the Museum of Mankind
6 Burlington Gardens
London W1X 2EX

Contents

Country and People 9

Daily Life and Subsistence 13
Food and water 13
Camp life 17
Tools 21
Water craft 22

Religion and Social Life 24
Totemism 24
Ritual and the sacred objects 25
Death and the after-life 28
Magic 30
Political and social organization 32
War 35

Trade and Exchange 37

Art 39

The Tasmanians 44

Further References 47

Grateful acknowledgement is made to the following for permission to reproduce photographic illustrations: P. J. Trezise (frontispiece); Axel Poignant; the Australian News and Information Bureau; Macmillan, London and Basingstoke. All the artifacts illustrated and the painting (Fig. 3) are from the collections of the British Museum and were photographed by the Museum Photographic Service. The drawings (except Fig. 15) are by Brian and Constance Dear.

Illustrations

Rock-shelter painting. Laura District, north Queensland *Frontispiece*

Map of Australia 8

Fig.1 The Macdonnell Ranges, central Australia 10

2 A man from Melville Island 11

3 Tunnawinnawate, a Tasmanian aborigine 11

4 Harpoon fishing from a dugout canoe. Arnhem Land 12

5 The spearthrower and its use 14

6 Boomerangs 15

7 Returning boomerangs 16

8 Making fire with the fire drill 18

9 A decorated basket from Arnhem Land 20

10 An axe and three knives 21

11 The *tula* and its use 22

12 Double raft of the Worora. Kimberley District, Western Australia 23

13 Ceremonial headdress of the Aranda of central Australia 25

14 An Arnhem Land corroboree 26

15 A stone *churinga* of the Ngalia tribe, central Australia 27

16 Rock painting associated with love magic. Arnhem Land 29

17 Methods of using the pointing bone 31

18 Clubs 33

19 Shields from Queensland 34

20 Shield from Western Australia 35

21 Shields from south-east Australia 36

22 A bark painting illustrating a myth. Arnhem Land 39

23 A painting of a fish in 'X-ray' style. Arnhem Land 40

24 A drawing on bark from Victoria 41

25 A ceremonial ground prepared for totemic rites. Central Australia 42

26 Model of a Tasmanian boat made from bundles of bark 44

Country and People

About half of Australia lies within the tropics. About two-thirds is desert or semi-desert; only the remaining third can be considered fertile. The variation in annual rainfall is more significant than the annual average: at Alice Springs, in central Australia, annual figures have ranged from a little over 1 inch to 40 inches.

A belt of mountains, the Great Dividing Range, runs down the eastern side of the continent. It intercepts the moisture carried by the south-east trades and therefore has a high rainfall, but it is the main cause of the aridity of most of the interior. The extreme south-west is well watered and fertile. Much of Australia, especially in the west, is plateau country at about 2,000 feet. A considerable river system, the Murray-Darling, drains the western slopes of the Great Dividing Range and reaches the sea near Adelaide. Elsewhere rivers are few and short. Not one flows into the Great Australian Bight.

In the arid interior watercourses are usually dry, though after rain large areas are flooded. Many drain into inland basins such as Lake Eyre, which most of the time are dry salt pans. With summer temperatures of 100°F (37°C) evaporation is very rapid, but the south-east winds can be cold in the winter. Most of the desert areas have some scanty vegetation, which bursts into flower after the rare rains. With higher rainfall tussock grasses increase and scattered trees and shrubs appear, merging into savannah woodland (Fig.1). Tropical rain forest is found in the Cape York Peninsula, and temperate forest further south on the eastern slopes of the Great Dividing Range.

It has been estimated that the population before the arrival of Europeans was about 300,000, a figure which emphasizes the inhospitality of much of the continent. The aborigines are usually of medium height and slender build, wiry rather than muscular, with little subcutaneous fat. Hair is usually dark brown to black and varies from straight to wavy or curly. Skin colour is medium to dark brown. Eyebrow ridges tend to be prominent, and the root of the nose depressed (Fig.2).

Their homogeneity in physical characteristics, including blood groups, suggests that the aborigines derive from one ancestral stock rather than from successive immigrations of differing peoples. They presumably came from Asia at a time when sea levels were lower than those of today and certain land bridges existed which do so no longer. Their nearest relatives seem to be

Fig.1
The Macdonnell Ranges, central Australia. This scenery is typical of much of the interior. Inedible wild pumpkins can be seen in the foreground.

Fig.2
A leading man of the Tiwi of Melville Island, off the north coast. The plaited bands on his arms indicate that he is in mourning and subject to certain taboos.

Fig.3
Tunnawinnawate, a young Tasmanian from the Cape Grim district. From a copy, made by his son Alfred, of a painting in watercolour by Thomas Bock, probably executed in the early 1830s.

some peoples of central and south India and the Vedda of Ceylon.

The extinct Tasmanians seem to have been generally similar in physical type. It used to be believed, on the basis of certain apparently negroid characters (such as hair form), that the Tasmanians represented a survival of an earlier Melanesian population of Australia or that they had reached Tasmania directly from Melanesia by sea; but recent research suggests that they derive from the same basic stock as the Australian aborigines, the differences being explicable by prolonged isolation. The last full-blooded Tasmanian died in 1876 (Fig.3).

The antiquity of man in Australia is firmly established. At Lake Mungo in western New South Wales a group was living a life similar to that of the recent aborigines of the same district about 32,000 to 25,000 years ago. They had a variety of flaked stone tools, suitable for preparing animal and

vegetable food and working wood, similar to those which were used on the mainland up to about 6,000 years ago and in Tasmania into the nineteenth century. They also, apparently, practised cremation. Man was at Koonalda in South Australia by about 20,000 B C, when he was using a limestone cave opening from a 200-foot sink hole as a source of flint for making tools. At about the same time or even earlier edge-ground stone axes were being made in the Northern Territory, millennia before the technique appears in the record elsewhere. (All these dates have been obtained by the radio-carbon method.)

The earliest radio-carbon dates for human settlement in Tasmania obtained so far are about 6,000 B C from sites on the north-west coast, but it seems likely that many earlier sites have been covered by the rising sea level. Tasmania was almost certainly populated much earlier than can be proved by evidence so far available (see p.46).

In more recent times there have been two main points of contact with the outside world. One was Cape York, where the natives were in touch with the islanders of Torres Straits and so with the 'Neolithic' cultures, based on cultivation of root crops, which predominate in the rest of the Pacific. The presence in the Cape York Peninsula of outrigger canoes is clear evidence of Melanesian influence, but the aborigines did not adopt cultivation and except in the immediate locality the effect of Melanesian culture seems to have been slight. The north-west coast and Arnhem Land have been visited at least since 1803, and probably much earlier, by Indonesian fleets in search of sea-slugs (*bêche-de-mer*) for sale in the Chinese market. These visits were short and seasonal, and no permanent settlements were established. Nevertheless Indonesian influence on the mythology, languages, and religious beliefs of the Arnhem Land and Kimberley aborigines seems to have been appreciable. Indonesians also introduced the dugout canoe (Fig.4) and the sail, but their influence did not penetrate far beyond the coastal fringe.

The first recorded sighting of Australia was by the Dutch Captain Janszoon who in 1606 made a landfall on the west coast of Cape York and sailed into the Gulf of Carpentaria. He was followed by other Dutch sailors from their bases in the East Indies, including Tasman in 1642. In 1699 William Dampier recorded accurate and valuable observations of the aborigines.

As a result of these voyages the northern, western, and parts of the southern coasts were fairly well known by the end of the seventeenth century. It was not until Captain Cook's visit in 1770 that the fertile and well watered east coast was seen by Europeans. This is the only part, except for a fairly small area in the south-west, which was obviously attractive for European settlement.

In some of the settled parts of east, south-east, south and south-west Australia the aboriginal culture has been extinct for more than a century. Elsewhere only a few aborigines still lead a nomadic life, though those settled at missions or government stations often disappear into the bush for several weeks or months. In many cases tribal organization has broken down, and younger men rebel against the authority of their elders and the restrictions of the totemic cults. The assimilation of the aborigines into white Australian society is proceeding, but with varying degrees of success.

Fig.4
An Arnhem Land aborigine using the harpoon from a dugout canoe.

Daily Life and Subsistence

The material equipment and the way of life of the Tasmanians differed somewhat from those of the mainland aborigines, and are described separately (p.44). What follows refers to the mainlanders only.

Food and water

The aborigines depended entirely on wild foods for their subsistence, the men hunting or fishing, the women collecting vegetable foods, honey, insects, shellfish, and other small creatures. None of them cultivated food plants (though some would replant pieces of wild yam), and their only domestic animal was the dog. In the arid districts they had to move continually according to the seasonal availability of food and water. Where nature was kinder it was necessary to move camp less frequently and for shorter distances. But there were no permanent settlements though favoured camping sites would be reoccupied at the same season year after year.

The weapons used in hunting are spears (often thrown with a spearthrower), throwing sticks and boomerangs. The aborigines are expert at tracking and stalking game and knowledgeable about its habits, and even in open country are often able to approach to close range.

The simplest spears are made from a sapling, the point of which is hardened by charring. Sometimes the head is barbed. Heads consisting of stone flakes are used locally and in the Kimberley District of Western Australia beautifully finished heads of chert or chalcedony (in recent times of bottleglass or porcelain) are fashioned by an advanced pressure-flaking technique, small flakes being pressed off with a bone tool. In south-western Australia a row of small quartz flakes was set in vegetable resin below the head. Spears with several heads are made for spearing fish, and on the north coast harpoons are used for catching turtles and dugong (Fig. 4).

The spearthrower has the effect of adding an extra joint to the arm and increases the power and accuracy of the throw (Fig.5). At the end opposite to the grip is a projecting peg which fits into a hollow in the butt of the spear. It was used over most of Australia but was absent locally, for instance in much of southern Queensland.

The weapon most characteristic of Australia is the boomerang. The hunting and war boomerang usually has a fairly uniform curve and a flattened section with sharp edges, and varies considerably in proportions and weight. It does not return; it flies in a straight line, rotating rapidly, and will break limbs or inflict gashes (Fig.6).

The returning boomerang (Fig.7), which is used by men and boys in exhibitions of skill, is lighter than a hunting or war boomerang. The angle between the two arms often approaches a right angle; the arms are in slightly different planes, like a propeller, and the section is plano-convex (⌒). It is thrown, spinning rapidly, into but at a slight angle to a light breeze. Its course curves across the wind, rising gradually, until it momentarily becomes almost stationary at the highest point (though still spinning); then it descends on a curving course to the thrower. The flight may be more complicated, in the form of more than a complete circle or a figure of eight. There are records of a returning boomerang being thrown over a flight of duck, which mistake it for a hawk (because of its hovering at the highest point) and dive down into a net stretched across a water channel, but otherwise it has no practical use. The returning boomerang is unique to Australia.

Fig.5
The spearthrower. (*Above*) A man of the Aranda of central Australia hunting with a spearthrower; (*below*) a spearthrower from Gippsland, Victoria, showing the grip and method of use.
1925 1–3 1

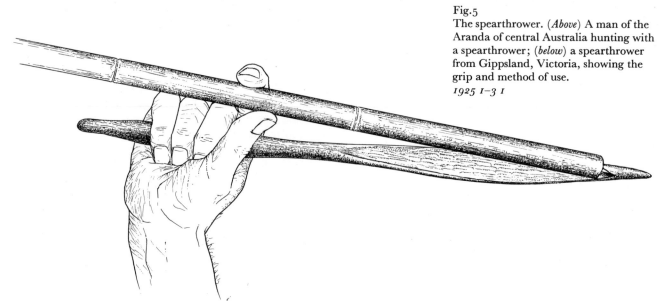

Fig.6
Boomerangs used in war and hunting.
(a) Aranda, central Australia.
1903 4-4 75
(b) Warramunga, Northern Territory,
used for throwing or held in the hand for
striking.
1903 4-4 173
(c) MacKay district, Queensland.
+ 5619
(d) West Kimberley district, Western
Australia. Boomerangs of this shape are
sometimes made to return.
99-441

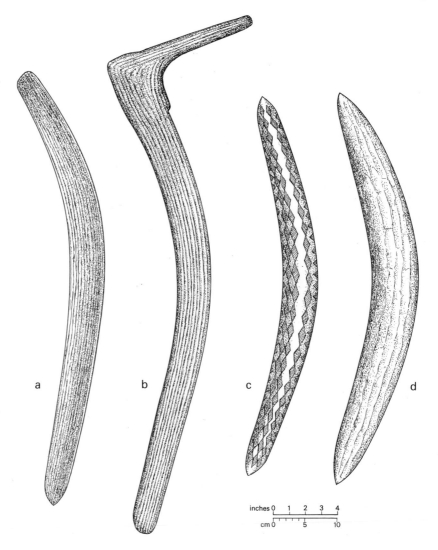

a   b   c   d

inches 0 1 2 3 4

cm 0   5   10

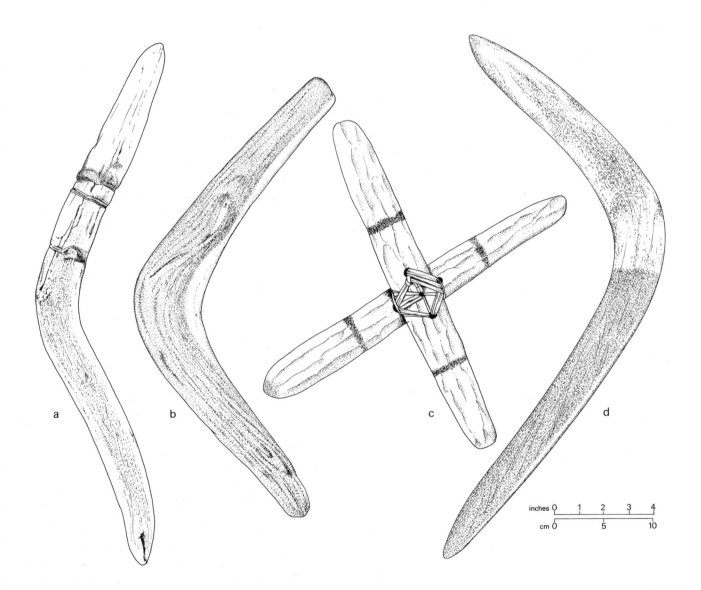

a   b   c   d

inches 0 1 2 3 4

cm 0 5 10

Fig.7
Returning boomerangs.
(a) Swan River district, Western
Australia, showing a native repair;
collected in the 1830s.
39 6–20 12
(b) South-eastern Australia.
(c) Cross boomerang, used for practice by
boys; Cairns district, Queensland.
1933 4–3 10
(d) Cairns district, Queensland.
1933 4–3 16

Nets are used for catching wallabies, which are driven into them, and funnel-shaped traps are set in gaps in a brushwood fence built across a wallaby track. In general, however, the aborigines do not rely greatly on traps. Where game is plentiful drives are organized, and grassland is fired to flush small animals.

The women's universal tool is a digging stick, a sharpened stake about 4 feet long which is used for digging up roots, grubs, edible ants (some have a sweet taste) and burrowing animals. It is also the weapon used in quarrels.

Fish hooks are simple and relatively uncommon. The making of weirs or pounds to catch fish, however, was widely practised. Extensive stone weirs with compartments from which fish could not escape were built in rivers of the Murray-Darling system. Simple funnel traps of basketry are employed to catch fish and eels; and water holes or river pools are 'poisoned' (drugged) with *Derris*, *Acacia*, or *Terminalia* species.

In the more arid parts movement is largely governed by the need to find water. There are permanent water holes in rocky formations, and water can sometimes be found by digging in certain parts of dried-up watercourses. If such sources fail it can be obtained from various roots and succulents. A species of frog, which stores water in its body and buries itself in clay during the dry season, is dug out and squeezed dry.

Camp life
Because settlements are not permanent, aboriginal shelters are flimsy. At a temporary camp windbreaks of branches or brushwood are erected. If the soil is sandy a sleeping hollow is scooped out and the soil banked up as a windbreak. On cold nights small fires are kept burning, and dogs and their owners huddle together for warmth.

Windbreaks provide little shelter from rain. Rock overhangs and the mouths of caves have been used since very early times. Sheets of eucalyptus bark were used to make shelters from Victoria to the north coast. Sometimes they are supported by a framework of poles, or large sheets are folded down the middle and set up on the ground like an elongated tent. In Arnhem Land and Cape York, where easier conditions make a more sedentary life possible, the wet-season bark shelter is raised as much as 6 feet on poles and a fire is kept burning beneath it to discourage mosquitoes. In the more arid parts the

Fig.8
Making fire with a fire drill. The vertical
rod is rotated rapidly between the hands
in a hollow in the softer 'hearth'.

typical shelter is dome-shaped, made by pushing branches into the ground in a circle, drawing their ends together and covering the whole with brushwood, grass, leaves or reeds, sometimes daubed with mud.

In the absence of fire-proof vessels cooking is confined to baking or roasting. Small animals and vegetables are roasted at the edge of a fire. Larger animals are cooked in a hollow scraped in the hot ashes and covered with embers and hot sand. The seeds of a number of plants are ground on flat stones into a sort of flour, made into cakes, and baked in the ashes.

The ability of the aborigines to utilize every resource is illustrated by the way in which the people of the Mann Ranges of central Australia obtain *kurrajong* seeds. The *kurrajong* grows in the desert where even the aborigines dare not go for lack of water. Crows, however, fly out to feed on the *kurrajong* and return to the water holes in the evening. The aborigines collect their droppings and by rubbing and winnowing separate the seeds, which are ground and made into cakes.

The making of fire depends mainly on the friction of wood against wood. The most widely spread method is the fire drill, in which a stick is rotated between the hands in a hollow in another piece of wood, usually softer (Fig.8). The fire saw, found mainly in central and eastern Australia, consists of a piece of soft wood across which a splint of harder wood is worked rapidly to and fro. The softer piece is sometimes split so that the wood particles fall through on to tinder beneath. In central Australia a softwood shield sometimes serves as the lower member and the edge of a spearthrower as the saw. By either method the smouldering powder is added to tinder – dry grass or other readily combustible material – and this is carefully blown until a flame appears. Percussion methods of making fire (by producing a spark) have been recorded, but it seems likely that this was copied from the flint and steel of the early settlers.

Their nomadic life makes it impossible for the aborigines to carry many goods with them. Their utensils are light and not easily damaged, and often have more than one function. The wooden bowls used throughout Australia serve for taking the products of a day's foraging back to camp, for fetching water, for carrying babies or personal possessions on the march, for removing soft soil when digging for food or water, for winnowing seeds to separate the rubbish, and for many other purposes. Some are made from a sheet of eucalyptus bark prised off the tree and further shaped by heating over a fire. Others are cut from solid wood.

Most aboriginal groups also have plaited bags or baskets. String bags are used for carrying personal belongings. The string is made by rolling vegetable or animal fibres on the thigh or with a simple spindle. Special bags are made to contain *pituri*, an indigenous plant which is chewed as a stimulant and is traded over long distances. Basketry techniques, for which unspun vegetable fibres are used, are employed to make bags and baskets for various purposes. Pandanus or palm leaf baskets, made not by plaiting but by folding the leaf and sewing or pinning it at the ends, are found as far south as New South Wales. In the north, where a more sedentary life is possible, baskets and bucket-shaped vessels are made from 'paper-bark' (from a species of eucalyptus) and large containers are made by folding a rectangular sheet of bark and sewing up the sides. These baskets are often painted (Fig.9).

Many aboriginal groups went naked, and it is probable that all did so before the influence of Europeans and, in the north-west, of Indonesians made itself felt. On coming into contact with Europeans most aborigines adopted some form of breech clout. In the southern part of the continent skin cloaks were worn, but for warmth, not modesty. They were usually made from kangaroo or opossum skins. These were dried, the inner side was scraped and fat was rubbed in. They were then sewn together with sinew. The inside of the cloak was often decorated with painted or scored patterns. They are now rare, partly because they were often buried with the dead. Various sorts of small tassels or string aprons are worn as pubic covers, and in parts of the north women have substantial matting skirts or aprons.

Ornaments for daily use are relatively few and simple, the more elaborate being mostly worn in ritual contexts. Necklaces are made from teeth, seeds or lengths of reed. Bone, wood, or reed pins are worn through the pierced nasal septum. Neck or waist bands of human-hair or vegetable-fibre string, the latter often coloured with ochre, may either be simple ornaments or have sacred or magical connexions. It is often difficult to distinguish between sacred and profane, for similar objects may have different connotations in neighbouring tribes.

The aborigines did not practise tattooing, but patterns of raised scars were formed by making cuts and rubbing in ashes so that they healed as weals.

Fig.9
A painted basket from Arnhem Land, probably from the Port Essington district. 18 in. (47 cm). *1939 Oc 8 37*

Fig.10
Tools.
(a) Axe with stone blade from the Daleburra of central Queensland. The haft is lashed with kangaroo sinew and the blade is further secured with a mixture of beeswax and vegetable resin. These are used for general woodworking purposes, occasionally for fighting, and for opening hollow trees to catch opossums and obtain honey.
1904 10-2 11

Tools

The essential tool throughout Australia was the stone axe (Fig.10a). The blades were made from large pebbles or from blanks of hard stone from which flakes were struck off, and except in the south-west the edge was usually finished by grinding. Boulders in which grooves have been worn by sharpening stone axes are common. The haft was made by bending a split stick, made flexible by heat, round the blade and binding it tightly immediately behind it. The junction was usually reinforced by moulding vegetable resin round it. In south-west Australia small, crudely formed axe blades were hafted by being set in a lump of resin at the end of a stick handle.

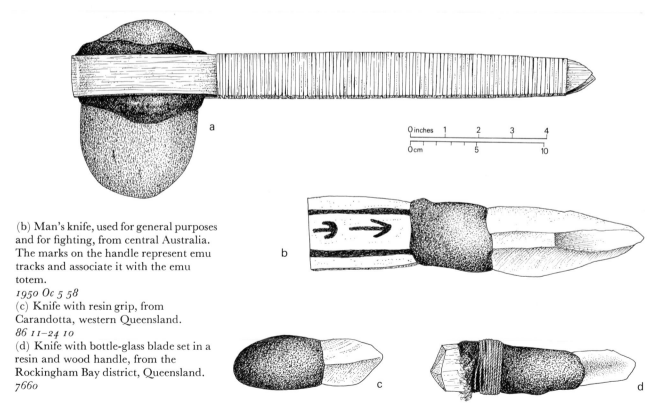

a

0 inches 1 2 3 4
0 cm 5 10

(b) Man's knife, used for general purposes and for fighting, from central Australia. The marks on the handle represent emu tracks and associate it with the emu totem.
1950 Oc 5 58
(c) Knife with resin grip, from Carandotta, western Queensland.
86 11-24 10
(d) Knife with bottle-glass blade set in a resin and wood handle, from the Rockingham Bay district, Queensland.
7660

b

c

d

These were used for cutting toe-holes when climbing trees. The methods of hafting are not very efficient, and blades need frequent resetting.

Another important tool found over a wide area of central and south Australia, the *tula*, consists of a sharp-edged flake set in resin on the end of a wood handle. This is used with a chopping motion (Fig.11) to hollow bowls or to make the longitudinal grooves typical of many wooden artifacts. It thus fulfils the functions of an adze, but can also be used as a chisel or gouge. Smaller chisels or gouges are similarly hafted.

Large flakes are used as knives and scrapers. A handle is made from resin moulded round the butt, or of wood secured to the blade with resin (Fig.10b); or the butt of the flake may be wrapped in skin. The knives are used for fighting or for general domestic use. For many purposes a suitable flake is held unhafted in the hand and discarded after use. The usual method of shaping stone tools is by percussion with a hammer stone. In south-western Australia knives were made by setting a row of small flakes in resin on a wood handle.

Kangaroo teeth are used for smoothing spear shafts or sharpening the points. Shells are used as scrapers or knives in coastal districts, and bone awls are found almost everywhere. Bone has many uses. In northern Queensland a tool made of sharks' teeth set in a wood handle was used for skinning and cutting meat and also as a weapon.

The resin used widely in hafting and for setting teeth or other materials to make ornaments is obtained from a number of plants: porcupine grass (*Triodia pungens*), grass tree (*Xanthorrhoea* sp.), wattle and eucalyptus species, and others. The leaves, stems, or roots are burnt or heated so that the resin exudes. Beeswax is used for similar purposes.

Water craft

The aborigines often make use of logs as floats when crossing rivers, and small children are floated across on sheets of bark controlled by swimmers. Rafts of several types are used. In the Kimberley District poles are pegged together to make a pointed raft, and two of these are used in conjunction, with the pointed ends overlapping (Fig.12).

All truly traditional canoes seem to have been made of bark. On the rivers of the Murray-Darling system oval sheets up to 20 feet long were removed

Fig.11
The *tula*, a tool which serves as both adze and chisel. The example shown, with relatively broad stone blades set in resin at each end, is used as an adze for working down the surface in making such articles as shields and wooden bowls. It comes from the Dieri of Cooper's Creek, east of Lake Eyre in South Australia.
1908 6–20 41

Fig.12
A double raft of the Worora, Kimberley District, Western Australia. The two sections are laid overlapping and are held together in the water by their own weight and that of the passengers.
1936 10–30 1

from large eucalyptus trees, and were further shaped by heating over hot ashes. The largest would carry six or seven people. Since the bark was removed from only one side of it the tree survived, and many such can still be seen. A different method is used in the tropical north. Here two horizontal cuts are made round the tree about 10–20 feet apart, and these are joined by a vertical cut. The whole of the bark between the horizontal cuts is then levered off (which kills the tree). The sheet is laid on the ground. At each end the sides are brought together and sewn with vine or bark strips to form the bow and stern. The sides are usually strengthened with poles laid along the gunwales, and rope or vine cross-braces are added to prevent the sides opening. The seams and lashing holes are sometimes caulked with resin. The aborigines are not a seafaring people, and canoes are used mainly on rivers or estuaries or for fishing in coastal waters.

Religion and Social Life

By contrast with their very simple material culture, the religious ideas of the aborigines are relatively sophisticated and their ritual and social life elaborate.

Totemism

The basis of aboriginal religion is belief in mythical beings, who in the beginning moved about the country fighting, hunting, and forming the natural features (but they are not creators: the land already existed). This formative time has been called the Dreamtime or the Dreaming – translations of terms used in some of the languages. These beings had the characteristics of both men and animals, which were then not distinct. A human group and an animal species share descent from one of them. The group therefore feels a special affinity with the species, which is their totem. In many cases members of the group are forbidden to kill or eat the totem animal, and they perform rites to promote its increase.

The Dreamtime heroes not only shaped the physical environment; they also by their actions set the precedents which for all time govern human conduct. On the proper observance of these rules of behaviour, as well as on the due performance of the rituals, depends the wellbeing of the human group and of the totem species too. The myths usually conclude with the Dreamtime heroes turning into rocks or animals or going to live in water holes, and losing individual physical existence, but their non-material essence survives and they are still actively concerned with human affairs.

The journeys and adventures of the totem heroes may cover large tracts of country occupied by more than one group or tribe, each of which is the guardian or 'owner' of a section of the myth and the sacred places connected with it. On totem affairs members of the totem can pass freely and safely through foreign territory. The mythology thus provides a cohesive force in a society composed of very small units.

However, totemism is a good deal more complex than a simplified account would suggest. Though animal species are the most usual totems, plants or inanimate objects may also be regarded in the same light. There are several other kinds of totemism apart from the form already described. Not all would be found in any one tribe. In some areas there are personal totems which act as guardians. These may be revealed in a dream, or a child's individual totem may be determined by the place at which it was conceived or born.

Fig.13
Ceremonial headdress, worn during totemic rites, from the Aranda of the Macdonnell Ranges, central Australia. 40 in. (102 cm).

There is sometimes a totem associated with each sex, which acts as an emblem and has various social functions.

Essentially totemism can be divided into two main forms. In one, the totem and membership of a social group are linked and totem affiliation governs marriage and sexual relations. The totem is inherited and there is a sense of blood relationship with the totem animal, which is not eaten except ritually. In the other the ritual aspect is emphasized rather than descent from a common ancestor. There is often no prohibition on killing or eating the totem, which is shared on the basis of the place of birth or conception. It may even be considered desirable that men and women who share the same totem should marry.

It has often been said that the aborigines do not understand physiological paternity. This seems to be only partly true. In any case physical conception is of secondary importance to the entrance of the spirit. Spirits awaiting birth congregate at certain places, such as water holes, to which a woman goes when she wishes to conceive. Sometimes a spirit makes itself known (often in a dream) to the father. Some tribes believe these spirits to be those of the dead awaiting reincarnation, others that they are 'new' spirits sent by the Dreamtime beings.

Ritual and the sacred objects

Sections of the myths, the associated rites, and the sacred places and objects are kept secret from women and uninitiated youths. Formerly anyone not entitled to it who gained such knowledge, even accidentally, was in danger of being killed. Initiation is progressive, and not until middle age or later does a man learn the whole of the esoteric lore.

Initiation is usually accompanied by physical ordeals. Circumcision is practised almost everywhere except in the east and south-east. In most of the same area subincision (an incision into the urethra below the glans penis) is also practised. These operations are performed with a sharp flake. Teeth are knocked out in many districts. In some parts of Australia women also are initiated and may have their own sacred lore, sites, and objects.

The ceremonies are of two main sorts. In one, primarily instructive, the myths are re-enacted for the benefit of the initiates, the patterns of conduct are recapitulated, and the unity of the group is emphasized. In the second the

ceremonies are directed towards increasing the totem species, man reinforcing nature by ritual means. In both the participants paint their bodies elaborately and form patterns with birds' down stuck on with their own blood. Elaborate headdresses of sticks, string, and feathers are worn or similar structures are carried (Fig.13). The ceremonies are often protracted and consist of chanting or singing the myths or the songs connected with them, contemplating the sacred objects and explaining them to initiates, dancing, and miming the actions of the totem animal or the mythical being (Fig.14).

The sacred objects associated with the ceremonies are regarded with great veneration and are kept carefully hidden. The tribes of central and Western

Fig.14
An Arnhem Land corroboree. On the left are the musicians, one playing a *didjeridu*, the other two clapping sticks together in rhythm.

Australia have *churinga* (*tjurunga*), flat tablets of wood, or in parts of central Australia of stone, on which are carved or painted designs which symbolize the totem myths (Fig.15). They are usually from about 4 inches to 2 feet in length, but in the Western Australian desert may be up to 15 feet long. In the centre and west the design is usually incised and the *churinga* is often coloured with red ochre. Further north they are commonly painted with red and yellow ochre and white, and decorated with down stuck on with human blood.

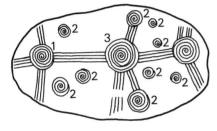

Fig.15
A stone *churinga* (sacred object) of the grasshopper totem, from the Ngalia of central Australia. The incised pattern recounts the totem myth (*see diagram above*). At a place called Ngapatjimbi (1) a number of grasshoppers came out of the ground, flew up into the air, and went into the ground again. There they multiplied, and after the next rain came out at other places (2). They flew into the air and came down as men. The men went to Wantangara (3) and, going into a cave, turned into *churinga*. The parallel lines represent the paths made by the grasshoppers by breaking down grass and leaves; the pairs of short lines are their prints in the sand. Ngapatjimbi and Wantangara are sacred sites in the desert about 50 miles north of the Macdonnell Ranges.
17 in. (43 cm). *1935 4–12 1*

Very similar in appearance are the bullroarers, which are always of wood. They too are usually carved with totemic patterns. At one end is a hole for the attachment of a string. When swung round they make a loud moaning or humming noise. The uninitiated believe this to be the voice of a totemic spirit, and so are warned to keep away while the rites are in progress.

Other sacred objects include carved and painted staffs, and rounded pebbles which are identified with the eggs or parts of the body of the totem animal (especially favoured in the north). 'Thread-crosses' – crossed sticks the arms of which are connected by cord, usually of human hair – play various parts in the ceremonies. Sometimes they are worn as headdresses or carried on the back by dancers.

A group of distinctive Australian artifacts which, although not usually sacred, are linked with ceremonial as well as with economic and social occasions are the message sticks. These do not have the same significance on all occasions or in all parts of the country. Usually they are from 2 to 12 inches long and often have notches or grooves cut into them. The stick is usually an *aide mémoire* to the messenger and is meaningless to anyone with no previous knowledge of the message. It may serve as a means of identification for an intermediary and ensure safe passage through dangerous territory. In some districts, however, they seem to be made in commemoration of notable events or to be used in magical rites.

Death and the after-life

The aborigines believe that few deaths are natural, most being caused by sorcery. Even when the reason is obvious – snake bite, lightning, falling from a tree, a spear wound – there remains the question to be answered: why did lightning strike *that* man? Why on this occasion did he lose his grip when climbing?

Most of the possible ways of disposing of the dead have been recorded in Australia. Burial is the most common, but cremation was widely favoured in the east. Some tribes expose the dead on a platform or place them in a hollow tree or rock shelter. Drying the body in the sun or over a fire was practised in parts of eastern and central Australia. These methods were often used in combination: for example, remains might be buried or cremated after exposure.

Cannibalism was often part of the mortuary rites, though rare in other contexts. The motives seem to have been pious duty and the acquisition of the dead person's qualities, and normally only selected parts were eaten. In central Australia a mother would eat her still-born baby so that the spirit might be reborn through her. Bones of the dead were made into necklets or the skull painted and carried about for a time before ultimate disposal.

Mortuary rituals, which both reconcile the living to their loss and send the spirit on its way satisfied, continue for some time. It is important that the spirit should not linger, for spirits can be malevolent. The camp is often abandoned and the dead person's possessions destroyed. Various means may be adopted to immobilize the spirit should it wish to work harm: the spear

Fig.16
A rock painting associated with love magic, from a site in the Wellington Range, western Arnhem Land, in Gunwingu territory.

arm of the corpse is tied, or its kneecaps removed. The survivors, and especially widows, gash themselves, smear themselves with clay, cut their hair, or observe a long period of silence. Among some tribes of western New South Wales and South Australia widows wore heavy caps of gypsum.

There are many views about the destination of the spirit, but it is agreed that conduct during life does not affect it: there is no conception of reward or punishment. The land of the dead is often in the sky, or among coastal peoples over the sea. Part of the spirit seems to remain in relics and to aid the living, part may become a malignant or mischievous ghost, part may return to a totemic centre to await rebirth. In general the spirit preserves its identity for a time and then merges with the spiritual forces of the Dreamtime. In this respect, as in others, beliefs vary and are often not clearly formulated.

Magic
Apart from the magical element in the increase rites, magic takes two other principal forms: sorcery or black magic, and healing or beneficial magic. The distinction is not always clear and all may be practised by the same individuals.

Beneficent magic includes love magic (practised by both sexes) (Fig.16), rain-making, healing and magic to avert misfortune or to give success in hunting or gathering. An important section relates to the 'inquests' which are carried out to determine the culprit when sorcery is suspected. The soil round a grave is carefully smoothed and examined for marks (made by small creatures) which show the direction from which the sorcerer operated. In the Kimberley district stones are placed beneath the platform on which the body is laid and the fluids falling on them indicate the source of the magic. On the lower Murray River the nearest relative slept with his head on the corpse so that he should see the sorcerer in a dream.

Sorcery often depends on the beliefs that it is possible to project magical power towards an enemy, and that it is possible to remove vital parts and close the wound magically so that the victim remembers nothing of what has happened.

One of the most common methods of magical killing is 'pointing'. The pointer is made of bone, or sometimes of wood, and is imbued with magical power by chanting. It is pointed towards the victim from a distance, to the

Fig. 17
Two methods of magical killing by 'pointing' as practised by the Aranda of central Australia: (*left*) using a pointed stick decorated with bird's down (from Baldwin Spencer and F. J. Gillen, *Across Australia*, vol. II, Macmillan 1912, Fig. 178); (*right*) using apparatus consisting of a number of bone points and two eagle-hawk claws attached to a length of human-hair string (from Sir Baldwin Spencer and F. J. Gillen, *The Arunta*, vol. II, Macmillan 1927, Fig. 120).

accompaniment of the prescribed curses, the user adopting a traditional attitude (Fig. 17), and acts like a magical projectile.

In central Australia when a revenge killing was planned a man was selected to 'go *kurdaitcha*'. He made a pair of shoes of emu feathers compacted with human blood and covered with a network of human-hair string, and had his little toe 'softened' on a hot stone and dislocated so that it projected sideways. Wearing the shoes, and accompanied by a sorcerer, he stalked his enemy and speared him. The avengers carried a *churinga* to give them strength. The wound was magically closed by the sorcerer and the victim was brought to life, unaware of what had happened, and returned to his camp where he soon died.

The full truth seems never to have been established. The shoes are certainly made (nowadays for sale to tourists), and it used to be fairly common to see men, their toes dislocated, who claimed to have been on *kurdaitcha* expeditions. Perhaps the belief arose from revenge killings with magical accompaniments in which the shoes were worn to prevent recognition of the killer's tracks.

There are related forms of sorcery in which the victim is believed to be captured by various means, his kidney fat removed, the wound closed and the victim freed to die soon after. There is no doubt such beliefs are firmly held and very persistent, and that those who believe they are the victims die. From a social point of view belief in sorcery is a strong sanction against breaches of the accepted codes of conduct.

Political and social organization

The word 'tribe' as applied to the aborigines has no precisely definable meaning, though most 'tribes' had names for themselves or were named by their neighbours and were recognized as groupings of some significance. They ranged in numbers from about 100–1,500 people. A tribe had a territory, and often, but not necessarily, a language or a distinct dialect. Usually marriage took place within the tribe; at least the tribe was potentially self-sufficient in this respect, unlike smaller groups which had to take their wives from outside. Members of a tribe have a sense of community, based on kinship (real or theoretical) and on attachment to the tribal territory and the mythology associated with it. But the tribe is not a political entity. Only on certain ceremonial occasions does the whole tribe come together, and even then members of other tribes may be present. It is the smaller groups which are the effective social, political, and economic units.

These smaller groups have a number of forms. Not all are found in a single tribe or area, but a tribe may have sub-groups of several kinds, functioning in different ways for different purposes. One type is the patrilineal local descent group, members of which claim common descent and share a territory and sacred sites, the men taking their wives from other groups. Clans, patrilineal or matrilineal, also claim common descent from a mythological or human ancestor, but their members may not be able to prove actual physiological relationship. Sometimes the clan has a defined territory, but members may be scattered, and the link totemic, not territorial. The basic unit everywhere is the family – a man, his wife or wives, and their children – which often moves independently.

Some tribes have a division into two exogamous sections called 'moieties': that is to say that men of each moiety take their wives from the other. The moieties may each be again divided into sections or subsections, men of any

Fig.18
Clubs.
(a) Victoria.
+ 2279
(b) 'Macquarie' (probably Port Macquarie), New South Wales.
94–285
(c) Throwing club resembling a boomerang; Dandaloo, New South Wales.
94–287
(d) Bogan, New South Wales.
94–291
(e) Daleburra, central Queensland.
1927 6–10 10

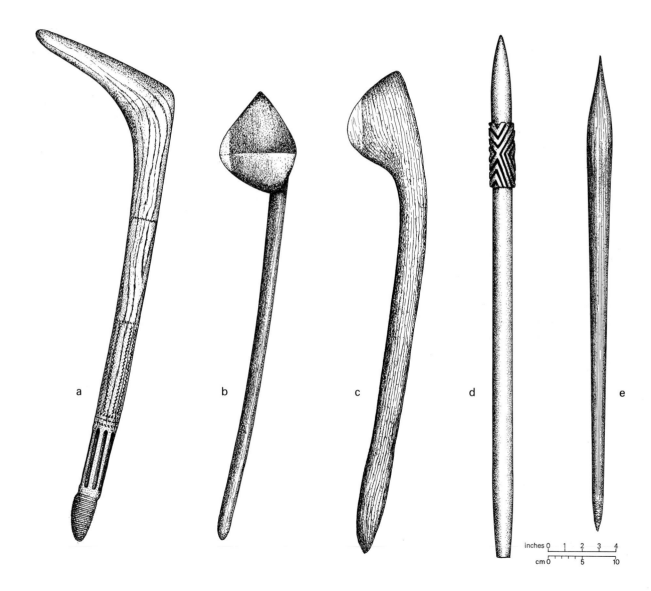

a   b   c   d   e

inches 0   1   2   3   4
cm 0   5   10

33

Fig.19
Shields from Queensland, painted with
totemic patterns.
(*Left*) from Rockingham Bay.
40 in. (101 cm). *7696*
(*Right*) from north-east Queensland.
50 in. (127 cm). *+2461*

Fig.20 (*opposite*)
Shield from the Hamersley Range
district, Western Australia.
45 in. (115 cm). *96–1024*

subsection of one moiety taking their wives only from one subsection of the other. Their children belong to yet a third subsection, in which moiety depending on whether moiety affiliation is by the male or the female line. Such marriage systems have a number of consequences. In theory a man marries his second cousin. In fact, in a small society, there may not be enough eligible women for the adult unmarried men. When two neighbouring peoples having different systems of this kind intermarry, even the aborigine experts are taxed to devise a workable reconciliation. Not all systems are so complicated, but prohibitions and prescriptions are always more numerous and more rigid than in a European society. In practice the systems can be manipulated to some degree, but latitude is severely restricted, and any gross breach of marriage regulations is regarded with horror and was punished by death.

The kinship system is a classificatory one: all kin of equivalent generation and status are addressed by one term (*e.g.* father's father and father's father's brother). This does not mean that there is in practice any confusion between a man's own brother and his father's brother's son whom also he addresses as 'brother'.

Monogamy is common, but not a rule. In some tribes the older men tended to monopolize the available women, but on their death the widows could be inherited by the husband's brothers or even by their sons.

War

The aborigines, who are not a warlike people, did not wage war with the object of capturing territory or achieving a defined political objective. Small-scale fighting, however, was not uncommon. The reasons were often connected with magical killing or revenge expeditions, with disputes about women, or with trespasses on hunting grounds or sacred places. In some circumstances formal duels were fought, and wrongdoers were killed by parties appointed for the purpose.

Many of the weapons used in hunting were used also for fighting. This applies to the majority of spears, spearthrowers, boomerangs and throwing clubs. Clubs for striking, which vary widely in form, were primarily weapons of war. They were always made of wood, but some tribes of central Australia had a war pick made from a stone flake mounted at a right angle to the haft.

Clubs with sharp edges ('sword clubs'), the effect of which is to gash rather than to crush, are found locally (Fig.18).

A form of boomerang which terminates in a hook (Fig.6) is apparently used as a war pick, as well as for throwing. It is said that when thrown the hook will catch on a weapon used to ward it off and the boomerang will swing round to hit the enemy. This type is found in the centre and north. War boomerangs tend to be heavier than hunting boomerangs and are often used for striking as well as for throwing. In north-eastern South Australia there are clubs shaped like a boomerang but too heavy to be thrown.

Shields, which are used only in war, have a wide distribution but are absent from some localities. In central Australia they are typically small, oval, of soft wood, decorated with parallel flutings, and coloured with red ochre. In north-eastern Queensland shields are much larger, and the front surface is not carved in relief but is painted with totemic patterns (Fig.19). Relatively long and narrow hardwood shields from north-western Australia have zigzag flutings in relief on the front surface, emphasized with red ochre and sometimes with yellow and white (Fig.20).

The most varied shields are those of south-east Australia (Fig.21). Here there were two types: a narrow, often deeply keeled form used for parrying blows from clubs and boomerangs; and a larger thinner form for parrying spears. The latter are made from thick hard bark, or are cut from wood, with handles carved from the solid, like most other Australian shields. Shields of both types often have incised patterns of closely spaced meandering or zigzag parallel lines which are sometimes regularly arranged to form rhomboids, and they are sometimes coloured in addition. It is noticeable that the grips of shields are nearly always too small to fit a European hand.

Trade and Exchange

Fig.21
Shields from south-east Australia.
(*Left*) from Victoria, used for parrying
clubs or boomerangs.
34 in. (86 cm). *1820*
(*Right*) the type used for protection from
spears.
44 in. (112 cm). *1950 Oc 4 10*

Certain kin exchange gifts, and goods are presented in connexion with
marriages, in compensation for wrongs, to those who control or arrange
ceremonies and on other social occasions. Game and other resources are
normally shared, the apportionment being laid down by custom. People who
gain a reputation for the manufacture of a certain kind of artifact make them
for exchange with others, but there are no whole-time specialists. The
mechanism of exchange varies from formal presentation to group exchange
and individual barter.

Trade often results from the local absence of essential materials. Stone axe
blades, for example, travelled over long distances. In some cases it is the
finished article that is traded; in some the raw material; in others (ochre is
an example) people come from a distance to collect the material and make a
payment to the owners of the source. Objects obtained from a distance
sometimes seem, by that fact, to acquire value or effectiveness or magical
power. There is a famous source of red ochre at Parachilna in the Flinders
Range of eastern South Australia. The ochre was said to have been coloured
by the blood of a mythical dog, which gave it particular potency, and it was
sought by tribes hundreds of miles away in south-west Queensland, although
they had much nearer sources. As long as trading parties kept to the
recognized route they were usually safe, and they could probably expect
protection from people of the same totem among tribes on the way. Groups
wishing to open trading operations at a distance would sometimes send an
emissary, who carried identification, such as a message stick, to ensure
safe conduct.

Items were more often traded from tribe to tribe, so that in any locality
the people knew neither the source nor the ultimate destination of the objects
passing through their hands. It was in this way that the incised oval pearl-
shell plates made in the Kimberley District of north-west Australia reached
the coast of South Australia, the extreme west near Exmouth Gulf, the central
western deserts, and Arnhem Land. It was not only material objects which
travelled. Non-sacred songs and dances (corroborees) were a form of
disposable property. Men were sometimes sent to distant tribes to learn a new
corroboree, which was performed by people to whom the words of the songs
were meaningless. Plotted on a map, the trade routes form a network. From
the point of view of an individual tribe, they themselves were the centre

from which the routes radiated. The constant contacts of people and movement of artifacts provided a means for the comparatively rapid diffusion of practices, ideas, and beliefs, of which circumcision and subincision are examples.

Fig.22
Bark painting from Oenpelli, western Arnhem Land. It was collected in 1948 by C. P. Mountford, who recorded the myth which it illustrates.
A couple with several young children lived near the waterhole in which dwelt Ngaloit, the rainbow-serpent. The parents died, and a man named Wirili-up undertook the care of the children; but he shirked his responsibility and gave them only a few nuts to eat. The children, hungry, were always crying, which so annoyed Ngaloit that he flooded the whole countryside. Wirili-up escaped by running to the plateau but the children could only climb a tree, and were drowned. The place is still feared and avoided. The painting shows the children climbing the tree and Wirili-up cracking nuts for one of them.
53 in. (134 cm). *1966 Oc 6 1*

Art

The main inspiration of Australian art is religious. By no means all is connected with ritual – though much is – but the *motifs* and the occasions are mostly linked with totemism or at least with mythology.

The aborigines fully appreciate well proportioned and skilfully executed work, and even the simplest artifacts are carefully finished, but the most complex decoration is reserved for ritual objects. The wood and stone *churinga* and bullroarers of central Australia are incised with curvilinear patterns consisting mainly of concentric circles, meandering lines, pairs or groups of parallel lines, and sometimes the footprints of emus or other animals. Most of the elements are meaningless to the uninitiated and give an impression of abstraction, but in fact the whole pattern records a myth; often a succession of incidents (Fig.15). The *churinga* are prepared for ceremonies with white down stuck on with human blood; in the north this is often the only decoration. The wooden *churinga* and bullroarers of the western deserts, and sometimes spearthrowers too, are usually closely covered with parallel flutings or grooves in the form of squares and rhomboids, angular meanders, 'Greek key' and zigzags. The patterns are basically similar to those of the central deserts, the differences arising from a preference for curves in one area and angular forms in the other.

Perhaps the best-known manifestations of aboriginal art, because of their frequent appearance in art galleries, are the bark paintings of Arnhem Land (Figs.22, 23). They are often made on the inside surfaces of the bark sheets which cover the wet-weather shelters, and are therefore visible to all regardless of sex or status. Some, however, are made in connexion with boys' initiation rites and are kept secret. This art is now commercialized, though technically the standard remains high and the paintings are still mostly in traditional style.

There are two distinctive styles in Arnhem Land. The 'X-ray' style of the west shows the internal structure of animals: the skeleton, the alimentary tract, the eggs. The artist in fact paints reality as he knows it, not merely what he sees (Fig.23). In eastern Arnhem Land there is a good deal more detail. Lacunae are filled in with closely spaced cross-hatched lines in several colours. Many paintings show incidents of a myth or objects associated with it. The islands off the coast of Arnhem Land have their own generally similar but distinct styles.

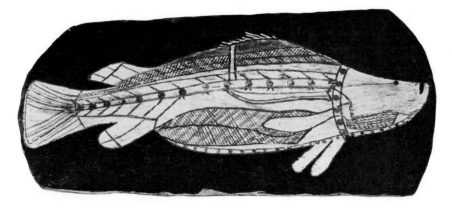

Fig.23
Painting on bark of a fish in 'X-ray' style from western Arnhem Land. 24 in. (61 cm). *1961 Oc 2 1*

Bark drawings of a different type are recorded from Victoria though very few have survived. The inner faces of the bark sheets forming the shelters became covered with soot, and the aborigines scratched drawings on the blackened surface. These seem to have had no ritual connexions (Fig.24).

Much of the most impressive art is in the form of engraving or painting on rock surfaces. The sites are usually rock shelters or shallow caves, protected from weather but in full daylight, for although much rock art was sacred and barred to the uninitiated the aborigines rarely worked in the depths of caves. Rock engravings or paintings, or both, are found throughout Australia except locally where suitable surfaces are lacking.

Engravings were made in several ways. In the soft sandstone of the Sydney district huge human or animal figures were outlined by cutting into the surface. Where the stone is harder, either the outline only or the whole figure is pounded, so that the pitted surface contrasts with the smooth rock face. In central Australia exposed rock surfaces acquire a brown patina against which the pounded surface shows white. Many engravings are of geometric or highly stylized *motifs*. Where the aboriginal culture disappeared before their meaning was recorded, or where they are ancient, it is possible to guess by analogy with similar markings elsewhere that these 'abstract' symbols are connected with totemic myths.

Although rock paintings are found throughout the continent, the art seems to have been, on the whole, less highly developed in the eastern part, though

Fig.24
A drawing on bark, probably from the Bendigo district of Victoria. The bark sheets from which shelters were made became blackened by smoke and the aborigines scratched drawings on the blackened surface. This is probably one of several exhibited in Bendigo in 1854 before being sent to an international exhibition in Paris.
25 in. (63 cm). *1827*

even here there are some notable sites (*frontispiece*). Certain simple styles and forms are widespread; these include outlines and silhouettes in monochrome, geometric or stylized motifs of uncertain significance, and stencils. The latter, most commonly of hands but also of boomerangs and other artifacts, were made by placing the hand or object against the rock face and spraying pigment over it from the mouth, so that the result is a negative stencil. The purpose, in some cases, seems to be to register the presence of the maker at a sacred site and to bring him *en rapport* with the Dreamtime beings.

Most painted figures are static. Paintings in which human figures with thin stylized bodies ('stick figures') are portrayed in intense activity, often in groups, occur in a wide area from Arnhem Land to the northern parts of South Australia and western New South Wales. In Arnhem Land, where they are overlaid by paintings in the 'X-ray' and other styles, and are therefore older, the present-day aborigines know nothing of their origin and ascribe them to tiny people called Mimi who lived in the rocks. In South Australia and western New South Wales the style survived into more recent times.

The rock paintings of Arnhem Land resemble the bark paintings of the same area. They occur in immense numbers, frequently superimposed one on another. Some sites are sacred and restricted to initiates; others are open to anyone. Some are associated with love magic or other magical procedures (Fig.16).

To the south-west of Arnhem Land, in the Kimberley District, is another distinct and well-known style, that of the Wandjina paintings. These are anthropomorphic figures, often very large and in groups, the most distinctive features of which are that they have no mouths and that their heads are often surrounded by radiating lines. The Wandjinas are Dreamtime heroes, each linked with a local aboriginal group but in a sense aspects of one being, and associated with clouds and rain. The aborigines believe that the paintings were originally made by the Wandjinas themselves and that their annual repainting revitalizes them and brings the monsoon rains, vital to man and nature.

In many parts of Australia the ground is modelled at the sites of initiation or increase ceremonies. Often this amounts to no more than making marks in dry soil or sand to represent the track of a totem animal, or drawing in it symbols connected with the myths, similar to those seen on *churinga*. The most

Fig.25
A corroboree ground prepared for a totemic ceremony in central Australia. The techniques of modelling the prepared ground and making patterns with ochre, birds' down, etc., can be seen.

elaborate examples are those of central Australia, where the soil is modelled in relief and covered with white and black patterns on an ochre ground. On this surface totemic patterns in birds' down are laid, using human blood as adhesive (Fig.25). Ritual stone alignments and cairns can be seen from Arnhem Land to Victoria.

An art form which reached its highest development in eastern Australia is the carving of patterns in living trees, usually made up of angular parallel grooves. The trees mark initiation grounds, or sometimes graves.

The dating – even the relative dating – of rock engravings and paintings presents great difficulty. Simple geometric or 'abstract' patterns have the widest distribution (including Tasmania) and must be very old. If one style is consistently overlaid by another, as in the case of the Mimi figures in Arnhem Land, then the former must be the older. The formation of patina over engravings or paintings, or the presence of cracks or displacement in the rock which clearly post-date their making, may suggest considerable age;

but such evidence can be misleading. Evidence is firm at Koonalda in South Australia, where flint nodules were being obtained from a cave 200 feet underground by about 20,000 BC. Here, partly covered by a rock fall which occurred early in man's exploitation of the site, and in complete darkness, there are parallel grooves and scratches in the soft limestone which must, it seems, be of human agency.

The pigment almost universally used in Australia is red ochre. Yellow ochre, black and white are also popular. Black is obtained from mineral ores or by crushing charcoal; white usually from clays. Pigment is ground and applied dry or mixed with water or fat. Brushes are made by fraying and teasing out the end of a stick or a strip of bark, or feathers are used. Fixatives, used especially on bark paintings, include turtles' eggs, orchid sap, and a mixture of beeswax and honey.

Museum collections inevitably give an impression that aboriginal art is almost confined to carving and painting; but there are many ephemeral forms of visual art: the decoration of the body, the preparation of ritual grounds, the flimsy objects connected with the totem ceremonies. Musical instruments are few and simple, being confined to the *didjeridu* (a tube through which a man sings, without words, found only in the north) and sticks clapped together to give time. But singing and chanting, the recounting of myths, and dancing and miming are dramatically and expertly performed. It is difficult for a European to appreciate the emotional impact of the ceremonies and the sacred objects on the aborigines, and their total absorption in their ritual life.

The Tasmanians

The material culture of the Tasmanians was the simplest to have survived into recent times. Nevertheless it represented an efficient use of resources at a low technological level; for the probable population of 3,000–5,000 had a density higher than that of most hunting and gathering populations of the modern world and comparable with that of the most favourable parts of the Australian mainland.

Their only weapons were spears and clubs. The spears were made from saplings or shoots which arose from stumps after burning; they were carefully straightened and the points were sharpened with a stone flake and hardened by fire. Clubs were usually about 2–2½ feet long, sometimes tapering slightly to the butt which was scored to improve the grip. The tip was usually rounded or pointed. Clubs were used for both striking and throwing, and sometimes for digging up roots or animals. Early accounts agree on the great accuracy of the Tasmanians in throwing spears, clubs, and stones.

Stone tools were not hafted but were held directly in the hand. They were made by battering or by percussion flaking, and the edges were often skilfully retouched. The techniques of grinding the working edges, as practised in most of Australia, and pressure flaking, were not known in Tasmania.

The only water craft were made from bundles of bark (usually three) lashed together. They were propelled by poling in shallow water, and in deeper water the poles, or perhaps pieces of bark, were used as paddles. They

Fig.26
A model of a canoe made from bundles of bark, the only sort of boat made by the aborigines of Tasmania. This model was shown at the Great Exhibition of 1851.
32 in. (81 cm). *51 11–22 3*

carried the Tasmanians across several miles of open sea to offshore islands to catch seals or birds or to collect eggs (Fig.26).

In the east, shelters seem to have been not much more than windbreaks of bark supported by sticks. On the west coast, with its higher rainfall, they were more substantial, being described as dome-shaped, 10 feet in diameter and about 7 feet high. The Tasmanians made simple baskets, and used shells or receptacles of kelp to hold water. Their only clothing was a skin cloak, and they had necklaces of small iridescent shells. They often dressed their hair with ochre.

Meat formed an important proportion of the diet. Large animals – kangaroos, wallabies, emus – were hunted mainly with spears. Family groups would combine to drive game to waiting spearmen or into water. Sharp stakes were apparently set in kangaroo trails, but no traps were made. Opossums were smoked out of hollow trees or caught by climbing, and birds seem to have been captured by hand from hides, using bait.

Any available berries, fruits, or roots were gathered. Women collected shellfish and other sea foods, including edible sea weeds; but for some reason the Tasmanians (unlike their ancestors 8,000 or more years ago) did not eat vertebrate fish. It is probable that the women's contribution to the food supply was more regular and more reliable than that of the men.

All the tribal groups had access to the coast. They also visited the central plateau where there are many lakes and water fowl were numerous, but they rarely entered the dense temperate rain forest which covers the mountains of the west, for the floor is carpeted with moss and animal life is scarce except in the inaccessible canopy.

It seems (though it is not certain) that the Tasmanian aborigines had no means of making fire, and they therefore preserved smouldering sticks with great care.

They were divided into loosely knit tribes, each of which had its own territory and sometimes a distinct language or dialect. Tribal territories were not rigidly defined and in the course of their seasonal migrations a tribe might cross the territory of another. Men seem usually to have taken their wives from other tribes. A tribe consisted of a number of families with their dependents, which were the effective economic units, but several such units or a whole tribe would combine for a special purpose such as a communal hunt or a ceremony. There were no chiefs, authority being in the hands of the older men.

Little was recorded of Tasmanian religious ideas. They are known to have feared evil spirits, especially in the dark, and to have held celebrations which included dancing. In this both men and women took part. They had myths concerning such topics as the origin of fire. It may be that their beliefs were of a totemic type, connected with the increase of food supplies, but there is no direct evidence. Cremation seems to have been the usual method of disposing of the dead, but they were also buried or placed in hollow trees. There is no record of cannibalism.

Every feature of Tasmanian material culture has a parallel in continental Australia. On the other hand the more specialized aspects of Australian culture are absent from Tasmania: the boomerang in all its forms, spearthrowers, shields, *churinga* and bullroarers, rock painting, and bark canoes are examples. The type of economy and the basic social organization, adapted to a nomadic life, are common to both, but the Tasmanians – as far as is known – lacked elaborate totemic rites, circumcision and subincision, and complex marriage and kinship systems. Their methods of disposing of the dead are all recorded from the adjacent part of Australia. The Tasmanians lacked the dog, which appears in the archaeological record in Australia about 7,000 years ago, after the separation of Tasmania by the post-glacial rise in sea level. The stone-working techniques and tool forms of the Tasmanians resemble those of early stone industries identified archaeologically in Australia.

No doubt further light will be thrown on Tasmanian origins as archaeological research expands in Australia and Tasmania. The evidence available at present suggests that after being cut off from Australia about 10,000 years ago, the Tasmanians preserved the basic culture of the first Australians, with little change, in almost total isolation.

Further References

Basedow, H., *The Australian Aboriginal* (Adelaide 1925)

Berndt, Ronald M. (editor), *Australian Aboriginal Art* (London 1964)

Berndt, R. M. and C. H., *The World of the First Australians* (London 1964)

Bühler, A., Barrow, T., Mountford, C. P., *Oceania and Australia: the Art of the South Seas* (London 1962)

Crawford, I. M., *The Art of the Wandjina* (Melbourne and London 1968)

Elkin, A. P., *The Australian Aborigines: How to Understand Them* (4th ed.) (Sydney 1964)

Mulvaney, D. J., *The Prehistory of Australia* (London 1969)

Roth, H. L., *The Aborigines of Tasmania* (2nd ed.) (Halifax 1899; reprinted Hobart, Tasmania 1968)